Iowa Fish Species

Game Fish & Panfish

Billy Grinslott & Kinsey Marie Books

ISBN - 9781965098899

Creek Chubs and Golden Shiners are two types of minnows that are considered panfish. There are several types of shiners. Many people will use them as bate to catch larger fish. Creek chubs are silver in color and golden shiner have a gold color. There are also many types of silver shiners.

Pirate perch, despite their name, pirate perch are not related to true perch and are the only living member of their own family. Pirate perch are primarily nocturnal predators, spending their days hidden among submerged roots and emerging at night to feed. They primarily eat aquatic insects and crustaceans but also consume other invertebrates and small fish.

Redear sunfish are known for their red or orange-edged gill flaps. They are a type of sunfish that thrive in warm, quiet waters, feeding primarily on mollusks and snails, and can grow up to 12 inches and weigh as much as 2 pounds. They are also known as shellcracker, due to their diet and the way they crush shells. The redear sunfish will thrive in most warm-water lakes and streams.

The Green Sunfish is blue green in color. It has yellow flecks on both its scales and some parts of its sides. The Green Sunfish also has broken blue stripes which is why some people confuse it with the Bluegill. Green Sunfish are very adaptable, they can live in any body of water that has vegetation or weeds. Green sunfish are opportunistic feeders, consuming insects, small fish, and other invertebrates.

Orange spotted sunfish are mostly found in floodplains of the United States of the Great Lakes. Its beautiful shiny silvery-blue body has reddish-orange spots, which give it its name, orange spotted sunfish. They are usually found in southern Muunesota but are too small to be popular with anglers. Their average length is 3 inches. They are a small fish.

The Warmouth is a member of the Rock Bass, Green Sunfish and Bluegill family. They can survive in low oxygen environments while other fish cannot. Warmouth can thrive in muddy water, when other fish can't. Warmouth are often confused with rock bass. The difference between the two is in the anal fin: warmouth have three spines on the anal fin ray and rock bass have six spines.

The bluegill also considered a sunfish is the most popular fish to fish for. They are called pan fish because they are about the size of a frying pan. Bluegills love to eat insects and bugs. They have good vision and rely on their keen eyesight to feed. Three types in this group are the Bluegill, Sunfish, and Pumpkinseed.

The Pumpkinseed is also known as pond perch, sun perch, and punky's sunfish. It can be found in numerous lakes, ponds, and rivers. It is their body shape resembling the seed of a pumpkin, that inspired their name. Pumpkinseed sunfish have speckles on their orangish colored sides and back, with a yellow to orange belly and chest. They are active during the day and rest at night near the bottom or in shelter areas.

River carpsuckers prefer large, silty rivers with slower-moving current over sand or silt bottoms but also thrive in smaller creeks and river areas. River carpsuckers are schooling fish and will often be found in large groups. They can grow to be 12 to 15 inches long but can reach a maximum of about 25 inches. River carpsuckers are omnivores, feeding on algae, detritus, plants, and invertebrates.

The two most famous perches are the common perch and the yellow perch. The yellow perch has a brilliant greenish yellow color with orange fins. The yellow perch is the biggest one and can grow to a size of 18 inches. It's also known as the jumbo perch. The other type of perch is the white perch. The largest yellow perch caught in Iowa, and the current state record, is a 16.4-inch, 2.79-pound fish.

The Rock Bass is not actually a bass but a member of the sunfish family. The biggest Rock Bass ever caught on record weighs about three pounds and was a little over one foot long. Rock bass prefer waters with rocky vegetated areas, that's how they got their name.

There are two main types of crappies. The white crappie and the black crappie. They are also members of the sunfish family. The difference between the white and black crappie is one has dark spots and the other has dark lines and is lighter in color. The white crappie has six dorsal fin spines, whereas the black crappie has eight dorsal fin spines. The white crappie can grow bigger and more of the bigger white crappie are caught in North America.

Sucker fish, also known as suckers, are freshwater fish with a unique sucker shaped mouth on the underside of their head. There are several types of sucker fish. Sucker fish feed off the bottom with their suction cup shaped mouth. The largest sucker caught in Iowa was a blue sucker, weighing 15 pounds, 6 ounces.

Redhorse fishes are part of the sucker family and are known for their bottom-facing mouths and fleshy lips which they use to suck food off the bottom. Redhorse has large, molar-like throat teeth that are an adaptation for crushing the shells of mollusks. redhorses construct nests in clean gravel, using their tails to sweep and their mouths to carry rocks or move materials with their heads.

Flathead Catfish, their body is wide but flattened and very low in height. Both eyes are on the top of the flattened head, giving excellent vision to see upward. Flathead catfish live mainly in large bodies of water like big rivers and reservoirs. They prefer deep pools. The largest flathead catfish ever caught in Iowa weighed 81 pounds and was 52 inches long.

The black bullhead and yellow bullhead are part of the catfish family. They usually only grow to about 10 inches long. They use their whiskers to help find food. The bullhead is the most common member of the catfish family. Bullheads live in the water containing low oxygen levels. They can survive on low oxygen areas, where other fish can't.

There are several species of catfish. The Channel Catfish are the most fished catfish species with around 8 million anglers fishing for them per year. Channel Catfish have very few teeth and swallow their food whole. Channel catfish live in freshwater rivers, lakes, streams, and ponds. Catfish can live in low oxygen water, like bullheads. The largest channel catfish caught in Iowa, a state record, weighed 38.13 pounds and was 40 inches long.

Bowfins can breathe both air and water, putting them at an advantage in low-oxygen waters. Bowfins are often described as prehistoric relics. This is because species can be traced to fossils from the Cretaceous, Eocene and Jurassic period. The largest bowfin caught in Iowa weighed 11.69 pounds and was 31.5 inches long.

Yellow bass, scientifically known as Morone mississippiensis, are a relatively small, schooling fish with a golden-yellow body and dark stripes, often found in rivers and lakes, particularly in areas with dense vegetation. The average size for this fish is 12 inches in length and one pound in weight. They are also known as rockfish, streaker, and yellow belly. The largest yellow bass caught in Iowa weighed 1.75 pounds. Length 14.50 inches.

Spotted bass have rows of dark spots on their sides and an iridescent green pattern along their back. Spotted bass are also known as Kentucky's or redeye bass. They are a popular game fish, often mistaken for largemouth bass, but they have subtle differences like a a smaller mouth. They are known for their aggressive nature and tendency to school together. They also prefer rocky bottoms and being in deeper water compared to other bass who like shallow water. The largest spotted bass caught in Iowa is a 2.06-pound (15-inch) fish.

White Bass range in color from a silvery white to a pale green. Their backs are mostly black, while their sides and belly are pale with stripes running along them. White Bass are related to Striped Bass and called wipers. The current Iowa state record for a white bass is a 5.11-pound fish. Length: 21.70 inches.

There are two different species of Gar, the Longnose gar, and Alligator gar. The Long Nose Gar got its name because of its long mouth that looks like an alligator's mouth. The alligator gar is one of the biggest freshwater fish growing up to 10 feet long. The world record for a catch was set at 327 pounds. The largest longnose gar caught in Iowa weighed 22.20 pounds and was 53 inches long.

Lake Sturgeons have sharp spines on their back, so be careful when handling them. Instead of scales, sturgeon skin is covered in bony plates called scutes, which can be very sharp on young sturgeon. Sturgeons have been around since the dinosaur days. Sturgeons mostly live in large, freshwater lakes and rivers. Their average lifespan is 50 to 60 years. The largest reported Lake Sturgeon caught in Iowa weighed around 100 pounds.

Shovelnose Sturgeons have sharp spines on their back, so be careful when handling them. Instead of scales, sturgeon skin is covered in bony plates called scutes, which can be very sharp on young sturgeon. Sturgeons have been around since the dinosaur days. Sturgeons mostly live in large, freshwater lakes and rivers. Their average lifespan is 50 to 60 years. The largest Shovelnose Sturgeon caught in Iowa weighed 12 pounds and was 33 inches long.

The burbot, also known as the eel pout. They get their name because they have a serpent-like or eel-like body. They can wrap their tail around things. There's nothing to worry about if you catch one, they may try to wrap their tail around your arm, but they are harmless. Burbots are adapted to cold water and are found in large, cold rivers, lakes, and reservoirs, primarily preferring freshwater habitats. Burbots are also known as eelpout, lingcod, and lawyer. The largest burbot caught in Iowa weighed 14 pounds, 3.6 ounces. Length: 37.25 inches.

Male freshwater drum make a rumbling or grunting sound by contracting muscles along their air bladder walls. They have large, ivory-like ear bones that can be up to an inch in diameter, which Native Americans used as necklaces or bracelets and sometimes referred to as the lucky stones. Freshwater drum are primarily bottom feeders, spending much of their time near the bottom of lakes and rivers in search of food. The largest freshwater drum caught in Iowa weighed 46.00 pounds. Length: 38.50 inches.

Buffalo Fish are sometimes confused with carp. Buffalo fish have a downward-facing mouth, capable of sucking bits of food out of the silt and sand on the bottom. They have broad bodies, blunt heads, and silvery gray or brown scales. Buffalo fish are members of the suckerfish family. The current Iowa state record for a Smallmouth Buffalo is a 43-pound fish. Length: 36.00 inches.

Carp have long been an important food fish to humans. Carp are bottom feeders for the most part and their mouth is made like a suction cup, so they can suck food off the bottom. Carp are good for a lake because they help clean the bottom of the lake. The largest carp caught in Iowa was a bighead carp, weighing 112 pounds. Length: 60 inches.

Brook trout are characterized by their olive-green bodies with pale, worm-like markings, red spots with bluish halos, and orange-red fins with white and black edges. They can grow up to 12 inches in length. Brook trout are cold-water fish that prefer clean, clear, and cold streams, lakes, and ponds. The largest brook trout caught in Iowa weighed 7.00 pounds. Length: 19.75 inches.

Brown trout can live up to 20 years. Brown trout have higher tolerance for warmer waters than either brook or rainbow trout. Brown trout can be found on almost every continent except Antarctica, and many can be found living in the ocean. The largest brown trout caught in Iowa weighed 15 pounds and 6 ounces. Length: 29 inches.

The rainbow trout gets its name because of its brilliant colors. Rainbow trout populations are good indicators of water pollution because they can only survive in clean waters. They like to live in rivers and streams. Rainbow trout rank among the top five most sought game fish in North America. The largest rainbow trout caught in Iowa weighed 19.5 pounds. Length: 35 inches.

Smallmouth bass have a smaller mouth than the largemouth bass. They also have different markings and are lighter in color. They don't live in most lakes because they prefer living in colder water. They are typically found in the northern states in America because the water is cooler. The current world record smallmouth is an 11-pound, 15-ounce fish caught in Dale Hollow Lake. The largest smallmouth bass caught in Iowa weighed 7 pounds, 12 ounces.

The largemouth bass is the most sought-after bass in North America. Largemouth bass live in just about every lake in North America. They have great hearing and can hear a crayfish crawling on the bottom of the lake. The largest largemouth bass caught in Iowa weighed 10 pounds, 14 ounces. Length: 23.5 inches.

The sauger is part of the walleye family. There are 2 different types of saugers. The normal sauger and the suageye. The saugeye is a mix of the sauger and walleye. The suageye have white eyes just like the walleye. The sauger and suageye are smaller than the walleye. Saugers are more likely to be found in large rivers with deep pools but are also found in lakes. The largest sauger caught in Iowa, and the current state record, weighed 6.50 pounds.

The walleye got its name because of its white looking eyes. Their eyes collect light, even in low light conditions. This means they can see in the dark. Because they can see in the dark, they mostly feed at night. During the daytime their eyes are very sensitive, so they usually head for deeper water or shady places. Walleye like to live in cooler water and are normally found in the upper part of North America. The current Iowa state record for walleye weighs 14 pounds, 8 ounces and measures 30.5 inches long.

The Northern Pike is one of the most sought-after fish for anglers. It got its name because it likes to live in cooler water mainly in the northern states of North America. The northern pike is a very aggressive predator. They don't like to live in groups with other fish, they are very territorial and like to live alone. Their behavior is closely affected by weather conditions. The largest Northern Pike caught in Iowa was a 25.31-pound fish, Length: 45 inches.

The muskellunge called the Musky or Muskie for short is one of the biggest game fish in freshwater lakes. The largest on record was 69 pounds, 15 ounces. The Muskie likes to live in cooler water and can be found in most lakes in the upper part of north America. Anglers look at Muskellunges as trophy fish. They are hard to catch, there's a saying that it takes a thousand casts to catch one. The largest muskellunge caught in Iowa weighed 50.38 pounds, was 52 inches long.

Fun Facts About Iowa Fish

1 - While Iowa Darter was considered for state fish status, Iowa currently has no official state fish.

2 - The largest fish ever caught in Iowa was a flathead catfish weighing 81 pounds and 52 inches long.

3 - Iowa is home to nearly 170 fish species, including primitive fish like paddlefish and sturgeon. This includes minnows.

4 - Lake sturgeon, a primitive fish with cartilage instead of bones, they are considered an endangered species in Iowa .

5 - Known as a scrappy-fighting, aerial acrobat, the smallmouth bass is considered the hardest-fighting freshwater fish.

6 - The Pondweed Killifish is the smallest fish about 1.5 inches.

7 - Trout are the only cold-water fish species in Iowa, with only the brook trout being native.

8 - Iowa law prohibits releasing Goldfish into public water, but you can use Goldfish as bait.

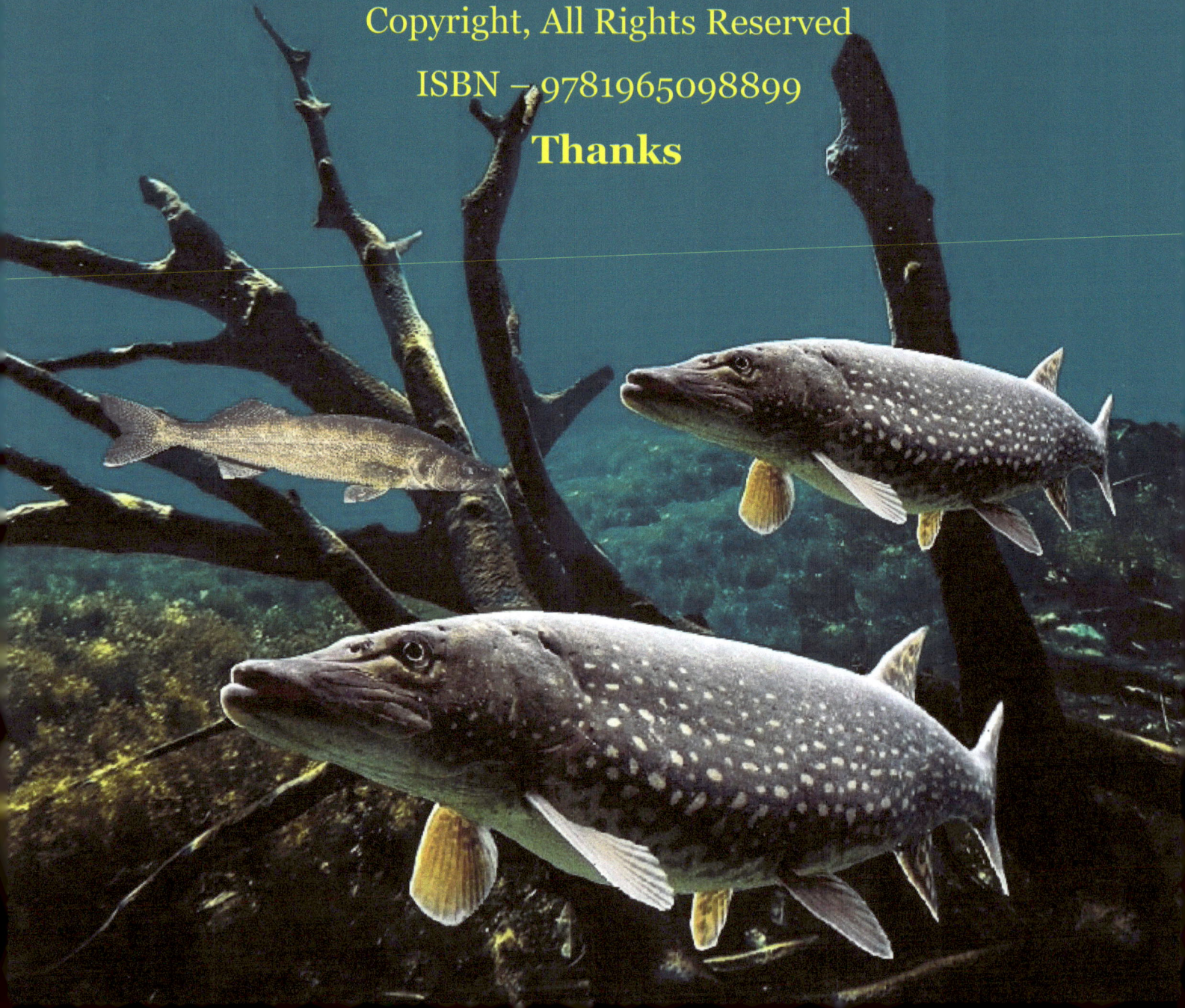

Author Page

Billy Grinslott & Kinsey Marie Books

ISBN – 9781965098899

Thanks

www.ingramcontent.com/pod-product-compliance
Lightning Source LLC
Chambersburg PA
CBHW060850270326
41934CB00002B/82

9781965098899